Broken Minds

R RADHAKRISHNAN

Published by Radhakrishnan R, 2023.

BROKEN MINDS

First edition. July 13, 2023.

ISBN: 979-8215118610

Written by R RADHAKRISHNAN.

Also by R RADHAKRISHNAN

The Mysore Triology
A Road less travelled

The Temples of India
The Temples of India: Somnathapura, Mysore

Standalone
The Colors of Life
The Temples of India : Guruvayur
Indian Mythology
The Book of Ancient Wisdom
Karna's Song
Artificial intelligence : AI for writers
Once Upon a Time: Traveller's Tales
Pen to Paper
Broken Minds

Watch for more at https://radhawrites.com.

To

Ganesha

and

Myself

Preface

Life is cyclic, nature is cyclic. After the scorching heat of summer, comes cool rains in the monsoon. From grief, we need to seek happiness.

The last couple of years have been traumatic for all of us. We lost friends, lovers, parents and so many loved ones. Grief is not just about losing a loved one, grief is about loss. Losing life, of friends, of jobs, or a way of life.

The most difficult part of my life began in 2020.

I retired, I moved, travel was curtailed, and we were stuck in a limbo. I lost friends, lost my parents.

My relationships with those I loved deteriorated and dark thoughts filled me.

I always loved words both to read and to write, but always there was a barrier, a hesitation to explore and let myself go.

The darkness built up inside of me and flowed out as words.

My mind broke and it let out the darkness, the sorrow that had built up inside.

It was letting out my grief in words that saved me from myself.

As I wrote, I saw hope. I saw the sliver lining in the clouds and I came back to life little by little.

For many of us, the times were bad and our minds were broken and our hearts damaged.

But life is cyclic. Unless we break, we cannot start afresh. We need to break the chains that fetter us. Unless Shiva destroys, Brahma cannot build.

A broken mind is the first sign of recovery. Embrace it, rejoice in it, examine it, and learn new dimensions in you and the world around you.

These are the words that helped me. They let the darkness out and I believe if we can find an outlet for the dark in us, we will overcome our sadness and learn to love life again.

I hope that these are words you can empathize with, that they touch a chord within you and help break your minds, set yourself free and choose life.

DARKNESS AND LIGHT
Vagaries of life
The mind frets
Worries of tomorrow
Yesterday's memories
Missing the present
Darkness dwells
Yet hope comes
Rising with the dawn
Light on my face
A lamp in my heart
Feeling the warmth
My soul stirs
Darkness lies dormant
Another day today
My soul stirs
Awakes in light

Live your life
What will tomorrow bring?
Heartache or Happiness
Sorrow and grief
Joy and wonder
Or will I?
Sleep in eternal peace?
Tomorrow is yet to come
Step up into the world
The soul is alive
Today and tomorrow.
R. Radhakrishnan
rr1krishnan@gmail.com
my website: radhawrites.com
Cochin, Kerala.

Shadow in my Soul

In the darkness
There is no light
Shadows in grey
A deeper darkness
Swirls within.
The canopy above
Of a moonless night,
The air is still
You sit and doze
As a mind numbs.
The moon flickers
You hope but fear
Silence stretches
The dawn is still
Far away, not near.
Fear holds your hand
Walking beside
Happiness is trending
We wear our masks
Cloak the despair.
Sadness is my shadow
Dull ache, my friend,
My eyes tell the tale
Of a soul lost
In the darkness of time.

Reflections regrets
Is a waste
Of energy and hope
I struggle mired
Swamped by thoughts.
The flickering lamps
The wavery light
The rise of hope
To crash on reality.
Shadows come to life.
No one to share
The darkness within
It is my own
My very own
Fattened, fed in the mind.

Virus Views

High up in Ivory towers
Sitting in protected bowers
Watching with tinted eyes,
While the world below cries,
The air is pure, I say
Save the world this way
Fear makes me blind
I see only the rind
Rotted fruit within
Masses bone and skin
Toil struggle and still
Empty bellies to fill
Work from home
Stop not to roam
Eyes glitter speak
Spirits grow weak
All I see are masks,
Oblivious to tasks
Beggar on the street
Kids with fleet feet
Cobbler on the corner
The tattooed foreigner
Begone and away
On fort walls only sea spray
Roads blank and forlorn

Vehicle where is your horn?
Life stands still
Tapestry yet to fill
The temple bells are still
Life flows on still
Clouds gather and swirl,
Thoughts are a whirl,
The darkness gathers
Over the land of our fathers,
What about our mothers?
But then who bothers
The roads are full of gaggle
Walking home to a fraggle
The ways are hard
Moving on a shard
Filling bellies on charity
The virus has no clarity
It reaches up high
There is no place to fly...

MIGRANT

I have seen death strike sometimes sudden and sometimes lingering, reluctant to take.

When it is sudden, it is always a shock, as it is unexpected.

Today a migrant worker died. A slab slid high up on a new building, trapping him between an iron rod and the slab as he hung outside on the scaffolding.

We watched him die.

It was traumatic and brought home a fundamental truth that we all are transient.

A friend and classmate sent a link to his podcast and the first one was on the need to share the love. His message was simple, sweet, and short. Please tell the people in your life that you love them.

Simple, yes, but most of us are so busy with the inanities of life that we forget. It is mostly the men who do this in India. They are so busy climbing up the career path or social ladder they ignore this. They always think they will make it up later, but that day may never come.

We look at migrants suspiciously, forgetting that many of us have been migrants or the other

We look down on these people and pass derogatory remarks and say he is not even from our country; he is from a neighbouring country.

But today I realized it did not matter where he was from. Like me, he is also a human.

He has come because of the need to live, because of his responsibility to his loved ones. He has not come to make life hard for me. He makes life easy for me by doing work I will not do. He has come as he has a hard life and he wants to work and live with dignity.

He has a family he loves. He probably never told them what they meant to him. Now he never can.

His origin does not matter, his language does not matter, his religion does not matter. All that matters is that he was a human striving for a better life.

A Migrant's Death

It hung swaying
The arms flapped
The head lolled
A puppet without strings.
Load on his back
He hung there
In pain
Screaming for help
In vain.
Family, food
Education, home
Children, parents
Siblings, marriage
Life's load.
A long road
A strange place
A better life
Dreams he had
Reality struck today.
High up
He worked
A slide
Slab of stone
On his back.
Humans watched

No one helped
Life squeezed
In pain
Slipped out.
In peace
He hung
Swaying gently.
They cut him down
Wailings afar.
Life went on
Just a migrant
Too poor
To matter.

Laughing away our fears

It is out there, the enemy
Of life, laughter, and love
It grips the heart with fear
It muddles the mind in rage
But I am among my friends
Surrounded by those I love,
We laugh at silly stuff
We never feel our age
We look fear in the eye
There is misery in loss
The heart mourns in tears
But we rally round
Together we will hold
We will laugh all we can
We will laugh our fears away.

A time of loss

The leaves are still,
The trees don't sway
The world is waiting
An eerie calm around
The sun sinks slowly
Every breath is pleasure
Who knows when it ends?
Men in arrogant Hubris
Owned the world
Ravaged the land
Nature was patient
She cajoled, she warned
Humanity was lost
The scourge unleashed
In droves, they died
Like flies, they dropped
Rich men, poor men
Great men, little men
The young and the old
Friends gone without a word
Leaving behind shocked fear
Boundaries make no sense
The invisible one strikes
High and low
In a random flow.

I sit in numbness
I sit struck dumb
I have no thoughts
In a bereft, bereaved mind,
I mourn for friends
I mourn for the loss
Frustration fuels anger
Helpless, I wait
For the next blow to fall
I hold to my heart
Friends and memories
Yesterday was light
Laughter in the sun bright
As darkness falls on my land,
I search my soul and mind
I yearn for the days of old
Friends whose hands I can hold.

Friendship

We were friends diverse
From child to adult
Good times and adverse
Together amidst tumult.
We were wont to laugh
At us and our faults
We were each other's staff
Safe in friendships vaults.
Politics peeped in
Debates and dissent
A virus within
Break-ups ascent
It is time to step back
Grow back the bond
Or the virus has a knack
Of damage gone beyond
Repairs or remorse
That serves no purpose.
These are troubled times
Difficult and perverse climes
Let us not be the Judge
Let us not hold a grudge.
Step back and move on
Life is more than dissent
It is easy to hate

Need to work on love
Don't leave it to fate

Need to work on love
Don't leave it to fate

FIGHTBACK

Loneliness in a crowd
Fear in the belly
Thoughts' turmoil
Sleepless dark
Toss and turn
Mind disarrayed
Rules to conform
Dawn is silent
Moments of peace
Crash of life
Tug of despair
Changes havoc
I push against
The tide threatens
Overwhelm, devour
Yet I abide
Spirit strong
Fight I will
The world to win.

Karna's Death

The wheel was in the rut
All I did would not avail
But yet I strained
All my life was a rut
But yet I abide
Struggle to survive
I would not surrender
To fate and destiny
To the end
To the end of days.
My brother stood
Bow in his hand,
Hate in his eyes
I bent my head
Shamed even at end
He set the arrow
His hand shook
I looked up
At Krishna's eyes
Compassionate smiling
My heart was filled
Love and peace
My search was to end
My brother's bow snapped
I watched death come

I smiled, offered myself
In peace, I lay
Unbroken, unbent.

Karna and Kunti

I stood in the light
The dark in me alight
Small, she stood straight
Red eyes on my face
My son, she whispered
My sin, I heard.
Krishna came too late
The truth, so frightening
She now stood before me
My heart exulted; mind numb
My mother, burden and sorrow.
Speech fled, thought died
Anger and sadness mingled
Harsh words I spoke
Love burst; regret flamed
I took that small hand.
She gripped with strength
Hugged me to her heart,
Tears washed my anger
Leaving love saddened
Truth is bitter, truth is anguish.
She tempted me
Brothers, family, kingdom, wife
Respect, repute, fame and glory
I smiled. I was her son too.

Firm would I be, in friendship
I put her away gently
I knew now my worth
A life was all I could give
But I gave her four lives
One would I take, I said
But in my heart, I knew
I was my own enemy
He was my brother
I could not take, only give
One life I had, that I would give
To my friend, my mother
I had nothing else to give.

KARNA and INDRA

I walked to meet the dawn
Golden rays on my brow
The war on the horizon
The brothers five in my sight
Years of slights, humiliation
Time now to pay in full.
My bow was stringed
Arrows sharp and straight,
The day had come
Retribution!
The Sun spoke in my mind
Retribution and revenge
Come around in circles
But I was firm for a fight.
An old man on the steps
Asking for alms in my way
My armour and earrings
He wanted my life in charity.
Sun whispering in my mind
Beware, Indra the sneak
Seeking favour for his son.
I laughed at Indra,
King of gods
Supplicant for his Archer son
My arrows still sheathed

I had already won!
I tore my armour,
Cut my earrings
Indra stood in shame
As they dropped into his hands,
His hands red in my blood.
Pain ignored; my spirit soared
Smiling, I bowed my head
You have made me immortal
Oh, Indra, lord of the heavens.
The shaft struck him true
He stood, his glory dim
Guilty and shamed
He offered me a trade.
Ask me a boon oh Karna
I laughed at that
I gave freely what you asked
I gave you alms, not a price.
Guilt, anger and shame
He shivered at his deed
I give you a boon, Karna
My Vajra, the thunderbolt.
I did not seek it
I did not want it
I had faith
In me and my arms.
But yet he was Indra
Lord of the heavens
I gave him the gift
Of redemption.
Indra laid the weapon in my hands
Unhappy and reluctant

Worried in his giving,
He still feared for his son.
Use it wisely, but only once
Indra was a miser still
His heart not in the giving
He set conditions and curbs.
I laughed at him
They called me low born
I knew not my mother
I knew not my father.
But my heart was true
My spirit still strong
I was a warrior true
Indra, shamed, sneaked away.

Karna's Soul

The soul shed its mortal coil
Broke the bonds that drag
It was twilight, harbinger of night
Yet I lingered, not fully free
Above that ground of death
Barren land drenched in blood
The body lay headless
Strong limbs asprawl
The head unblinking watched
Jackals tore the entrails
I felt not the pain
It was me for so long
Striding in strength
Alive across this land
My arms were strong
My shoulders broad
Benign Sun, my father
Watched as I grew
In strength and fame
And yet I felt that pain
A yearning to belong.
She came then, iron lady
Small, hard, emotions in thrall
She took my head in her arms
She sat forlorn in that field

My blood on her hands
She held the rotting flesh to her
She pulled that broken body
Hugged it like she would never let go
I was the soul, undying spirit
I felt not the bonds of Earth
And yet I felt her pain
They came together then
My brothers unknown
Hesitant, with dragging steps,
They watched their mother
Wail and weep over me
Their shattered faces
Distressed eyes, let me know
The pain they felt and the guilt
The Archer sat at my feet
His head drooped, and he sobbed
My soul felt that cry of pain
The others sobbed in grief
I could but watch their pain
I could share the sorrow
At last, I knew myself
It was time for me to go.

Ageing Grace

There is a turmoil within
An urge still to win.
A chip on the shoulder
In a world grown colder.
We walk with bravado
Strut like a desperado.
There is no empathy
Very little of sympathy
The outer core is hard
Inside, of fear, a shard
Life keeps laughing at us
As we debate and discuss,
We have grown in years
We have increased our fears
We still jump into the fray
Though our hairs are grey.
Life is all about living
It is not about proving
The race has been run
On the side-lines, watch the fun
It is time to forget frenetic pace
Time now to enjoy your place.
You may be number one
You may not have won
But still you ran the race

It is time now for grace
Gather your friends
Life still has bends
Watch the wonder
Take time to ponder
Governments will be there
They never will be fair
But you don't need their drivel
You have fought for survival
It is in you to win
Fight that turmoil within.

Abide, my friend

The sun sets in a rush
Twilight descends in a hush.
Death stalks in the air
Catching one unaware.
It is going to be a long night
Full of worry, anger, and fright
The darkness lies on the land
Threatening in a multiple strand.
Air hangs still, the wait is long
Need to keep our faith strong
This darkness will also end
The Sun, its light, will send
We will walk together, old friend
This too shall pass and end.
Together, we will watch that dawn
A Golden light falling on the lawn
We will clasp our hands
We will come from all the lands.
From the East, from the West
North and South, full of Zest
We will sit together to break bread
We will catch up on our life's thread
One day soon this nightmare will end
Till then abide and await my friend.

Hope

Silences awake
Soul within
Mind meanders
Random thoughts
Stillness seeps
Sleeping soul
Focused mind
Opened eyes
Cloister cacophony
Clutter mind
Round round
Aimless circles
Thoughts jump
Heart fears
Day follows
Night comes
Dawn dispels
Dark mind
Rays warm
On my face
Eyes closed
Step forward
Life awaits
Leap ahead!

Darkness

I fear the darkness
Inside and insidious
Gnawing away
Eroding the mind
The light struggles
Trapped in a corner
Anger rises
The darkness feeds
It is bright daylight
Yet the shadows grow
They numb my sense
The heart dreads
The mind flitters
Round and around
In dark alleys
Of shadowy thoughts
I give up the battle
Some days are like that
I pick up my pen
And shadows drip
Dark ink forms my words
Thoughts let out
Some relief from the dark
The light is lit as a spark.

A slow death

Lost in the dark
The devil is in me
Turbulence and trials
Emotions wreck
Relations break
Links forged weak
The mind numbs
The heart breaks
Woman I wish
You happiness
I wish you joy
Watch me die
Bit by bit
Chip away at my heart
Forget laughter
It has been long
Since I smiled.

Rage

The madness is on me
The darkness of the soul
The anger of loss
The fear of loneliness
The body falters
The mind drifts
Yesterdays are missed
The present is a misery
Existence without aim
The indolence of wait
The rage is there
Reined in tight
Fires burning me inside
The smile is a mask
Of the snarl within
The growls of rage
Silent screams
Of a bereft mind
A heart unwanted
Disposed after need
The rage builds up
I dam it tight
It rages to reach
The flailing tongue
Decades together

A waste of my life.

Once upon a time

Once upon a time
When I was slim
And yes, a little dim
Care free child
Playful a little wild
The child is lost
Adults pay a cost
The years take a toll
Often in ways droll
Twists and turns
As destiny churns,
The mind is jaded
The memory faded
Life is a circle round
Old mates are found
Gone are adult fears
As the child reappears
Once upon a time
Once more...

Night

Nights warm
Sleep oblivion
Rain pattering
A lullaby
Dreams die
Reality a pain
Morning dull
Aching head
Life floats around
A stagnant me
Left behind
Unwanted
Heart beats
Mind swirls
Eyes see
Darkness
Comes the knight
Steed of darkness
Relief and Rescue
A Good night

# The Broken Mind

The mind is dark
In complex knots
Pathways blurred
Meandering in dark
Heart beats in fear
No one is near
Lost that is dear
Twist and turn
Mind hold terror
In fetters grim
Dark and foreboding
Reality fades
Mind awakes
In darkness
Is peace
End it Soon.

The Broken Mind

Angst inside
Dullness death
Mind mindless
Eyes no sight
Heart in pain
Emotions churn
Fear fuels despair
Maze all around
Trapped mind frets
Morning is a haze
Rote is king
Body moves
Without mind
I am lost.

Revival

Lockdown silences
Fear fetters
Eyes hooded
Masked mouths
Rains lash
Whip broken lines
Flickering lights
Shivering trees
Silent crows
Croaking frogs
Darkness in light
Empty mind
Devils not kind
Phone pings
Old friends
Fear flees
Mind awakes
Spirits renew
Young again
Happy and free

Struggle at Sea

I kneel on the planks, body crouched
The sea foams as it slams the beach
The muted thunder of the waves
Fills my ears, spray stings my eye
My catamaran rises to meet the swell
I thrust my paddle and push
Forward I go a little bit
The wave passes, I wait for the next
The sea spins me round and around
Holding breath, I paddle and push
Forward I go a little bit
My raft spins as the waves slap
My body tired, my spirit strong
I meet the sea with paddle and prayer
Forward I go a little bit
The sea chuckles and turns back
I pull the net, the small fish struggle
Silver, they glisten in the morning light
The waves come to steal my catch
But fast and furious is my paddle
I stand up and brave the sea
I balance and pull in my catch
The playful sea lets me go
I kneel back and watch her go
It is cold in the morning light

The sun still not very bright
But I am soaked with sweat
My muscles all spent
I keep a watchful eye
When all seems over,
The sea may strike
I wait, watchful, fearful
The watchers on the beach
Silently watch, morning walkers
Out for a stroll on the beach
Watch me struggle for self and soul
At last, I meet the homing current
The playful sea carries me home
I land on my strip of sand
My brothers rush to help
We sit together, my brothers and me
Thin, unshaven, we smell of fish
The catch is lined on the beach
The fat ones come to haggle and preach.

Progressions

Gone is the child
Arisen a man
Free of fetters
Innocence and Ignorance
There he stands
In the doorway to fears.
New sensations, realizations
Steal inside
Gone is the old
Leaving behind
A sense of loss
Welcome the new
Grope and stumble
Rise up again
And again, and again...

Removing the block

Words jumble, clash
Thoughts run amok
To crash and smash
Alphabet and number
Jostle jump and mock.
Disturb my slumber
Wearily awake
Crowing cock
Coffee to make
Sun peeps wary
Cold shower shock
Day is now glary
Dress and rush
Ready for the crock
Words strive and push
Numbers crunch
Life is a rock
Bread to munch
Ashes in the mouth
What's today's stock
It's all going south
Enough and stop
Remove the block
Words gush
All in a rush

Hither and thither
Barriers smash
Broken tether
Mind soars free
Jumbled thoughts
Aligned and ready
Thoughts now flow,
Give ache a blow
Life is a deception
Of the mind, a perception

Happiness and Joy

Rain on the Roof
Puddles on the ground
Feeling in the mind.
Breeze on face
Hum of tires
Rustle of leaves
Heartbeats.
Smell of Earth
Touch your love
Hold her close
Breath in her hair.
Flowers in bloom
Child at play
Crow on the tree
Grinning at me.
Squirrels chattering
Love of a dog
Friends lost
Meet again.
It's yesterday
Child again
Siblings speak
A little touch
Kindred look
Happiness and Joy

Perception in the mind.

Loneliness

Alone in a crowd
Bereft abandoned
Heartaches, despair
Light sits the darkness
In a blank mind,
Moods swing
Tiredness, desolation
Tedium and silence
Talk on the surface
Smile in grief
Opportunities lost
In diversions
Chasing Mammon
Necessity for living
No-one understands
Hidden hurts
Tongue freezes
Society frowns
Forces combine
Relations end
Loneliness Kills.

Lost love

Life stood still
A void unfulfilled
She has gone
Forever somewhere
The stretch of eternity
The boredom of life
The feeling of hopelessness
A dream was she
A wisp of smoke
Enchantment
In absurd reality

Dawn

Dawn chill
Light glimmers
I close my eyes
Shadows shiver
Mind drifts
Aimless in fear
Alone in bed
Nothing to hold
No one to cuddle
Heat rises
Sun scorches
Getting up
Bones creak
Blood flows
I breathe
Another day
A search for light.

Karna battlefield blues

The Sun warm in its glow
Yet I shivered in the pale dawn
My life lay in shambles
I had lived a lie in the dark
The light I yearned for
Burns and blinds me
My life built on hate
My search in anger
The hate is gone
Despair in its place
The search has ended
Splitting my soul
Between a dear friend
And brothers new
Between my word
And what is right
Krishna smiles
He knows and understands
My mother wails
But not for me
The dogs howl
I step out into the gore
The madness of battle
It is time to end
Slip off the misery

I am alone but for my bow
Brothers ring me with hate
Friends, look to my victory
Expectations sag my shoulders
Perceptions sear my soul
The arrow comes with hate
It leaves me in peace.

Relationships

Illusions and dreams
Realities and perceptions
Relations and expectations
Happiness and sorrow
Fathers and daughters
Mothers and sons
Husbands and wives
Anger and hurt
Heart and soul
Sacrifice and grief
Pain and loss
Life is but death.

This Life

A vortex called life
A world in strife
Alone in the mass
Staring at the mess
The blank white wall
An empty mind
Drifting in the dark
The eyes speak
The mouth is shut
Life is a circle
Going nowhere
The heart beats
Emotions churn
Screams stilled
Trapped in rote
Struggles inside
Dead outside.

Memories

Memories are sweet sadness
That breech your defenses
Touch your heart
The past is gone
Lost in mists of time
Memories remain locked
In the vaults of the mind
Life is change
All that remains
Moments and memories
Strung together
Life moves forward
The past is gone
A faded picture
A sigh in the heart.

Anger

The darkness dwells
Hidden deep
In the mind
Patient and sure
When you relent
It slips your guard
A moment is all
The rage bursts
The fire sears
Relations snap
Life has no purpose
But hate and destruction.

Laughter

It is out there, the enemy
Of life, laughter, and love
It grips the heart with fear
It muddles the mind in rage
But I am among my friends
Surrounded by those I love,
We laugh at silly stuff
We never feel our age
We look fear in the eye
There is misery in loss
The heart mourns in tears
But we rally around
Together we will hold
We will laugh all we can
We will laugh our fears away.

Don't miss out!

Visit the website below and you can sign up to receive emails whenever R RADHAKRISHNAN publishes a new book. There's no charge and no obligation.

https://books2read.com/r/B-A-QDEN-XWPLC

BOOKS2READ

Connecting independent readers to independent writers.

Did you love *Broken Minds*? Then you should read *Indian Mythology*[1] by R RADHAKRISHNAN!

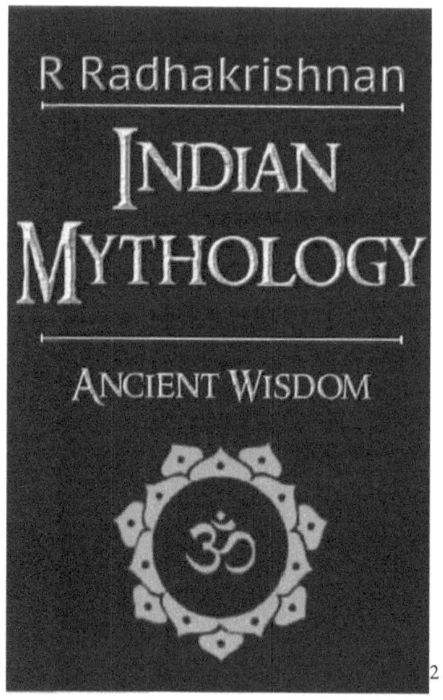

[2]

The Rishis, the wise men of ancient India, were in a dilemma. They had compiled the Vedas, the rules of behaviour, and Dharma had been conceptualised or framed.

Dharma, you could consider as a mission statement for life.

But how to reach it to the people so they could understand? How to ensure that people listened to the lessons? One of those wise men then came up with the brilliant idea of telling stories which would interest people and also have the required knowledge to learn from.

So were born the marvellous stories or epics of Hinduism. The stories have in them ideals, morals, rules of life and so much more. It brilliantly packaged these ideals in stories that enchant and yet teach.

---

1. https://books2read.com/u/mqE17Q

2. https://books2read.com/u/mqE17Q

This small book has some of those stories of ancient wisdom. R.Radhakrishnan retells and interprets those tales simply and links them to our everyday life. These are tales that gently guide even as they amuse you with thier wit and imagination.

Read more at https://radhawrites.com.

Also by R RADHAKRISHNAN

The Mysore Triology
A Road less travelled

The Temples of India
The Temples of India: Somnathapura, Mysore

Standalone
The Colors of Life
The Temples of India : Guruvayur
Indian Mythology
The Book of Ancient Wisdom
Karna's Song
Artificial intelligence : AI for writers
Once Upon a Time: Traveller's Tales
Pen to Paper
Broken Minds

Watch for more at https://radhawrites.com.

About the Author

Radhakrishnan, a seasoned traveler and storyteller, hails from Mumbai, India, and has explored various parts of the country during his three-decade-long career in a petroleum company. Being fluent in six languages has enabled him to connect with people and listen to their stories.

Passionate about narratives, Radhakrishnan has been exposed to a wide range of stories and their different versions throughout his travels, which significantly transformed his perspectives on life and India as a whole. His book, "Traveller's Tales Once upon a Time," set in the rapidly changing India of the 1970s, 1980s, and 1990s, offers captivating insights into a bygone era. With a delightful touch of humor and profound insight, these stories are sure to captivate and enchant readers.

Radhakrishnan's fascination with Indian mythology has led him to immerse himself in the ancient tales that have been passed down through generations. He heard these stories first from his parents and grandparents and later during encounters with many people during his journeys. These timeless stories embody the essence of India's soul, forming a living mythology in the ancient land. Radhakrishnan masterfully retells these tales, infusing simplicity and clarity while highlighting the invaluable life lessons they impart, lessons that remain relevant in the present day.

After retiring from Indian Oil, Radhakrishnan now dedicates his time fully to his passion for writing and traveling. His writing style is marked by simplicity, clarity, and empathy, effortlessly presenting complex ideas in concise and understandable ways. Occasionally, his emotions spill over, giving rise to stark and minimalist poetry, where profound thoughts and ideas are beautifully etched.

When not exploring India, Radhakrishnan lives in the picturesque coastal city of Cochin, Kerala, with his wife and two children. He maintains a blog titled **radhawrites.com**. Experience the artistry of Radhakrishnan's storytelling and embark on a journey through his vivid narratives, allowing yourself to be transported to the heart of India's diverse tapestry.

Read more at https://radhawrites.com.